THE ACTIVIT
BIBLE

THE ACTIVITY BIBLE

Stories by Su Box

Illustrations by Graham Round

Equipping the Church

Published in the UK by Equipping the Church, a brand of Kingsway CLC Trust,
Unit 5 Glendale Avenue, Sandycroft, Deeside, CH5 2QP.

ISBN: 9781803760179

Kingsway CLC Trust is a Charity, Number 265612, and a Limited Company
registered in England, Registration Number 1093879.

This edition 2024

Publishing Director: Annette Reynolds
Puzzle checker: Ben Reynolds
Art Director: Gerald Rogers
Pre-production: Kev Holt, GingerPromo

Printed in China

Presented to: ____________________

From: ____________________

Date: ____________________

Contents

Old Testament

New Testament

The Old Testament

God makes a world

At the very beginning of time, there was nothing. The world was dark and cold and empty. Then God spoke.

'Let there be light!'

Light shone in the darkness and God liked the light.

Then God made the day and the night, huge mountains, rolling hills and the deep blue sea.

God made plants and flowers and trees, stars and planets, the red-hot sun and the silvery moon.

God filled the sea with fish and the air with birds and made animals of every size and colour.

Then God made people, a man and a woman to look after His beautiful world. They were called Adam and Eve.

God looked at all He had made. He was pleased with His creation. It was a good world.

Spot the differences

There are eight differences between these two pictures. Can you put a ring around each of them?

Colour by numbers

Use the numbers below to make the butterfly beautiful.

1 Yellow | 2 Red | 3 Brown | 4 Blue | 5 Green

Everything goes wrong

Adam and Eve were very happy.

They chose names for the animals. They ate all the good things that grew in the garden. But in the middle of the garden there was a big tree. God told them they must not eat from that tree.

One day, a snake came and whispered in Eve's ear.

'Look at that lovely fruit,' he hissed. 'Go on, try it.'

Eve looked at the juicy fruit. She reached out and picked some. Then she took a big bite and shared the fruit with Adam.

Suddenly they knew that what they had done was wrong.

God had given them everything. He had only asked them not to do one thing – and now they had done it. They had disobeyed God and everything was spoiled.

Now God could not let them stay in the beautiful garden. Adam and Eve went away sadly. They could not return.

Find and count

Count how many times each of these things appear in the picture of the garden where everything goes wrong. Write your answer in the box.

Frog

Rabbit

Blue flower

Crocodile

Colour the dots

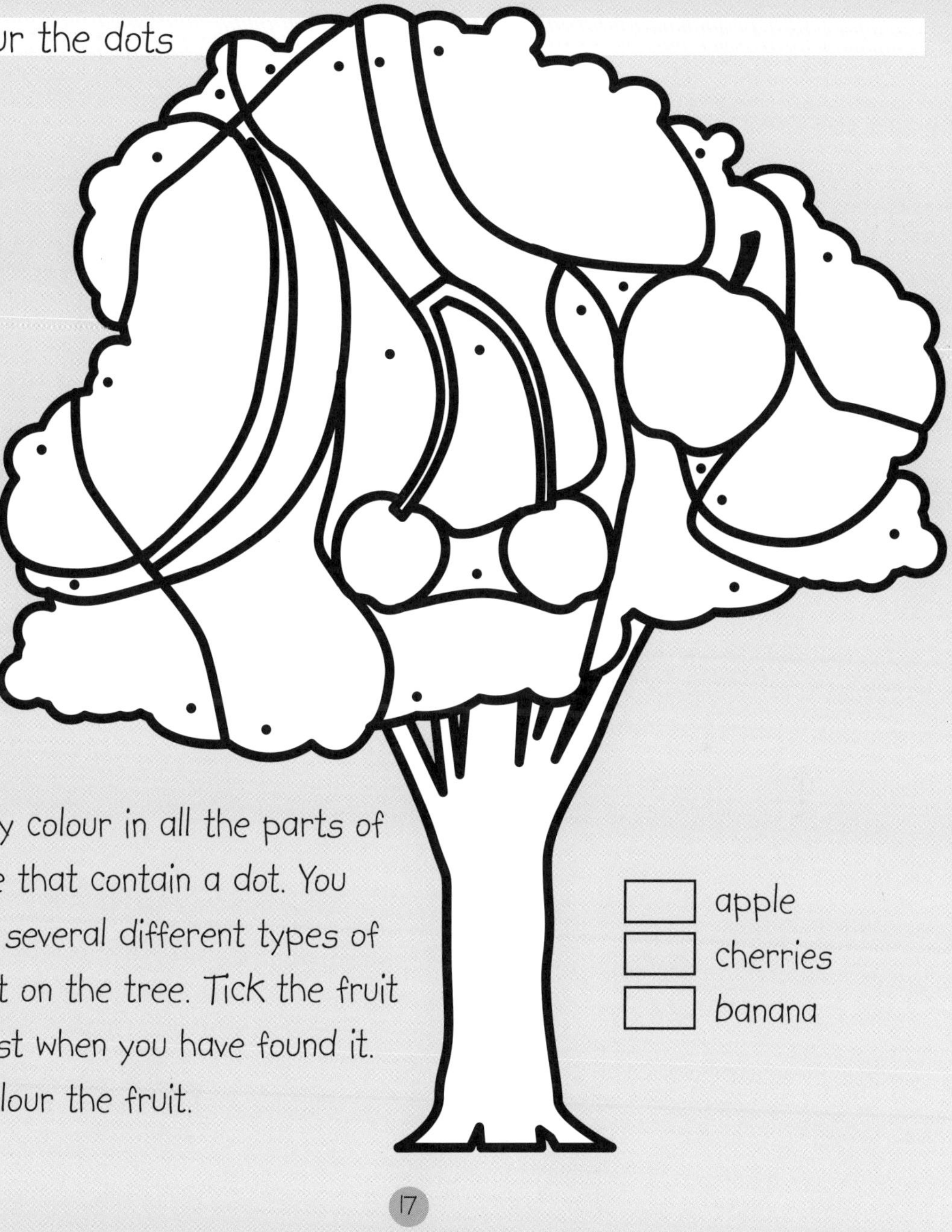

Carefully colour in all the parts of the tree that contain a dot. You will find several different types of fruit left on the tree. Tick the fruit in the list when you have found it. Then colour the fruit.

- ☐ apple
- ☐ cherries
- ☐ banana

Noah's ark

God was sad. The beautiful world He had made was no longer good. The people He had made hurt each other. Noah was the only good man left.

God spoke to Noah. 'I will send a flood to wash the world clean. But I will keep you and your family safe. Build an ark, a wooden boat large enough to take your family and two of every kind of animal, and cover it with tar to keep out the water.'

Noah built the ark and collected together all the animals as God

had told him. Then God shut the door.

Pit, pat, pit, pat, the rain began to fall. It rained all that day and all the next. Day after day after day, the rain fell down.

Match the pairs

The animals went into the ark in pairs, but some of them have lost their partner. Can you draw a line between the pairs of animals?

Wordsearch

The names of all the animals in the pictures are hidden in the grid of letters below. Put a line through each of them as you find them.

owl

horse

dog

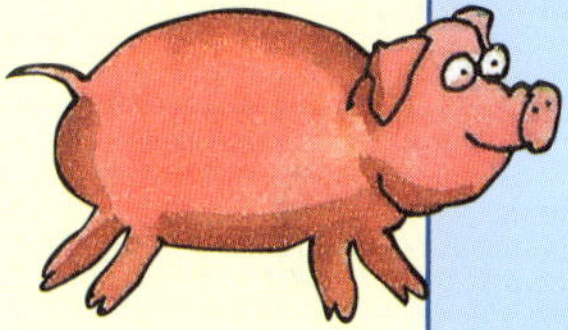

pig

a	g	h	p	w	v
l	i	o	n	x	a
f	m	r	p	i	g
o	a	s	m	d	a
x	p	e	o	w	l
d	o	g	v	w	m

fox

lion

Rain, rain and more rain

The puddles became streams and the streams became rivers. The rivers became great lakes until there was nothing left to see. Everything was covered by the flood waters.

It rained for forty days and forty nights. Then, one day, everything was still. Everything was quiet. The rain had stopped.

God made a strong wind blow until slowly, slowly, the flood waters began to go down.

The ark came to rest on a mountain.

'It is time for you to leave the ark, with your

family and all the animals, Noah. Go and make your home here again.'

Then the sky was filled with the colours of a beautiful rainbow.

'The rainbow will remind you of My promise never again to destroy the earth with a flood,' God said.

So Noah and all the animals lived on the land again and Noah thanked God for keeping them all safe.

Elephant in the maze

Now that all the animals have come out of the ark, can you help the elephant to find its mate?

Matching parts

Can you draw a line to connect the correct *backs* and fronts for each of the different animals?

Abraham moves to Canaan

One day, when Abraham was already quite an old man, God spoke to him.

'I want you to move from here, Abraham, and make your home in a new land. I will look after you and show you where to go. I will make your family into a new nation.'

Abraham trusted God. He took with him his wife Sarah and his nephew, Lot, and all his servants, sheep and goats. They travelled by day and made camp at night, sleeping in tents. Abraham went where God told him to go.

When they reached the valley of the River Jordan, Abraham and Lot decided to share out the land so that there would be plenty of room for their sheep and goats to graze on.

Lot went one way and Abraham stayed where he was. Abraham settled in Canaan, the land God had given him to live in.

Sheep sizes

Abraham had many sheep in his flock. Can you put a **B** next to the biggest sheep and an **S** next to the smallest?

How many sheep can you count?

Colour the picture

Colour in the clothes of Abraham and Sarah to complete the picture.

Baby Isaac

Abraham trusted God to keep His promise to make a nation from Abraham's family. But he and his wife had no children. Day after day, no baby came.

Then God spoke again to Abraham.

'Look up at the stars, Abraham. Try to count them! You will have as many descendants as there are stars in the sky.'

One day, three men came to visit Abraham.

'Come and rest and have some water to drink,' said Abraham. 'Have some food with us.' Bread was baked and meat was cooked for Abraham's visitors. He looked after

them well.

Then one of the visitors said, 'We will come back to see you soon, then your wife will be nursing her baby son.'

Sarah laughed to herself. Surely it was too late now for her to have a child?

But sure enough, nine months later, Sarah did have a son. They called him Isaac, which means 'laughter'.

Star puzzle

How many stars can you count in this picture of the night sky? ☐

Tick the star that is different.

Dot-to-dot puzzle

Connect all the dots, starting at 1 and ending at 31, to see what God gave to Abraham and Sarah. Then colour it in.

Jacob plays a trick

When Abraham's son Isaac grew up, he married Rebecca. They had two sons, twins called Esau and Jacob. Esau had been born first. One day, Isaac would give Esau a special blessing.

One day, Esau came home from hunting to find Jacob cooking.

'Give me some of that stew!' he said to his brother. He was very, very hungry.

'You can have some stew if you let me have your blessing for being the eldest son,' Jacob said quickly.

'You can have anything as long as I can eat now!' said Esau.

When Isaac was old and almost blind, he asked Esau to go out hunting so he could have his favourite meal.

'When you return, I will bless you before I die.'

Rebecca thought quickly. She cooked for Isaac, and made Jacob dress in Esau's clothes so he would smell like Esau, and tied goatskins on to Jacob's arms so he would feel hairy like Esau.

Jacob took the food to his father and Isaac blessed Jacob thinking it was Esau! Jacob had tricked his father.

Spot the difference

There are five differences between these two pictures. Put a ring around each one as you find it.

Esau's maze

Draw a line between Esau and the tent without crossing any of the red lines.

Joseph's special coat

Jacob got married and became the proud father of twelve sons and a daughter. He loved all his children but his favourite was Joseph.

One day, Jacob gave Joseph a beautiful coat to wear. All his brothers were jealous.

Joseph had strange dreams. He told his brothers about them the next day. But they didn't like what they heard! It sounded as if one day his brothers would bow down and worship him...

The brothers talked among themselves. They became more and more angry. Why did their father like Joseph the best? What would happen if Joseph were no longer there...?

The brothers wanted to get rid of Joseph. They waited for the right moment...

Colour the coat

Use your colours to make Joseph's coat beautiful.

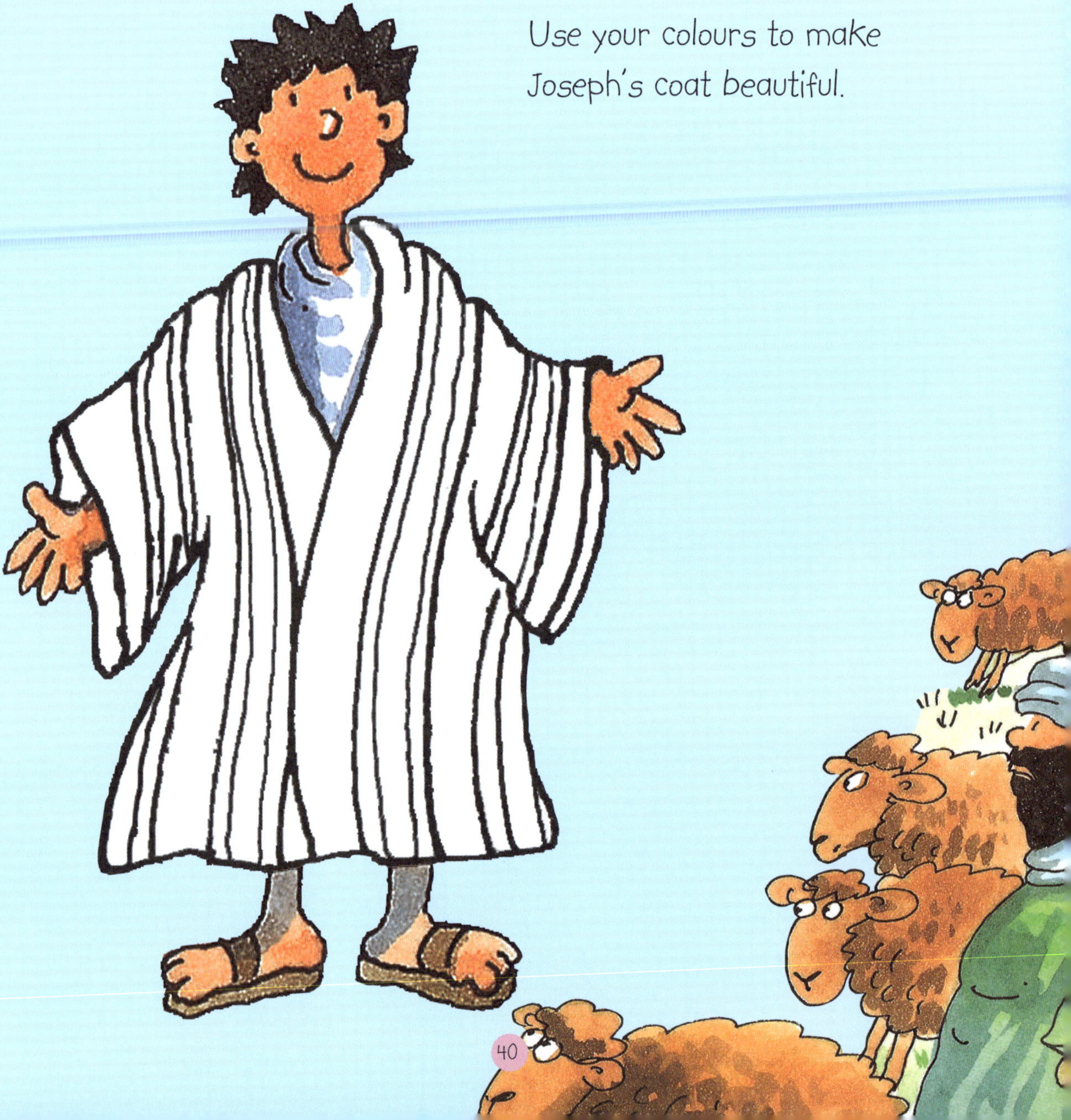

Counting puzzle

How many sheep can you count in the picture?

How many of Joseph's brothers can you see?

A slave in Egypt

Joseph's brothers were out looking after their father's sheep in the fields.

'Here's Joseph, that dreamer!' they said to each other. 'Let's kill him now and throw him into that dry well. We can tell Dad that a wild animal killed him. He need never know the truth.'

So the brothers grabbed Joseph, tore his beautiful coat off him, and threw him into the well. Joseph was stunned! What were his brothers thinking of?

Then a group of traders passed by on their way to Egypt.

'Let's sell him to the traders!' said the brothers.

So Joseph was sold as a slave and taken to Egypt. They dipped his coat in goat's blood and told their father that Joseph was dead.

But God had plans for Joseph. Years later, his dreams came true. When his brothers went to Egypt looking for food, they bowed down to the new ruler, second only to the king. It was their brother Joseph. So it was that Jacob and his family went to Egypt to live.

Find the birds

Coloured parcels

This camel is carrying a heavy load of parcels. How many of each colour is he carrying?

(red square)	Red	☐
(blue square)	Blue	☐
(yellow square)	Yellow	☐

There are six birds hidden in the picture above.
When you find them, mark them with a circle.

The baby in the basket

Many years later, the new King began to fear the number of God's people who lived in Egypt. First he made them his slaves. Then he told his soldiers to drown the baby sons of each Israelite family in the River Nile!

But one mother hid her baby. When the baby was too big to hide, she made a basket and put her baby in it. Then she hid the basket among the reeds on the River Nile.

Miriam, the baby's big sister, watched as the king's daughter came down to the river to bathe. Then the baby cried.

'A baby!' said the princess, picking him up.

'I know someone who can feed the baby,'

said Miriam, and she ran to fetch her own mother.

'Look after the baby for me until he is big enough to live in the palace,' said the princess, 'and I will pay you.'

The baby was called Moses. He grew big and strong and lived in the royal palace.

Catch a fish

The ibis is trying to catch fish to eat. Draw over the lines which go from his *beak* to a fish.

Connect the pairs

There are two of each of these things in the picture.
Draw a line between the pairs.

Let My people go

God had sent Moses to rescue His people from the cruel new king of Egypt.

'God wants you to let His people go,' said Moses.

'I don't know this God,' the king said. 'I will not let my slaves go.'

'Then terrible things will happen in Egypt!' said Moses.

First the water in the River Nile turned to blood. But the king would not let God's people go. Then the land was covered in frogs and biting insects. All the working animals became ill and died. Terrible boils appeared on the skin of all the Egyptians.

Hailstones pelted the land and locusts ate all the crops. Then the land went dark. There was no sun shining in the Egyptian sky. But still the King would not let God's people go.

Finally, the firstborn son of every family died.

The King of Egypt sent for Moses.

'Take your people,' he shouted. 'I will let them go.'

Adding up

Add up the number of frogs in each of these sums and write the answer in the box.

Odd one out

Three of these pictures of Moses are the same but one is different.

Write the number of the one that is different here. ☐

The great escape

Moses led God's people out of Egypt towards the Red Sea. God went in front of them by day in a pillar of cloud and by night in a pillar of fire.

But as soon as they had left him, the King of Egypt changed his mind.

'What will I do without my *slaves!*' he wailed. 'Get my war chariot ready. We must bring them back!'

God's people were trapped. The Red Sea was in front of them; the Egyptian army was behind them.

'Don't be afraid!' Moses told them. 'God will keep you safe!'

Moses held his stick out over

the waters of the Red Sea and the people watched as a path opened up for them so they could cross on dry land. Then Moses held out his stick again and the wind blew back the water to cover the path and the Egyptian army who were following. God's people were safe and on their way to the land God had promised them.

Strange sheep

Can you see what is wrong with each of these pictures? Put a circle around the mistake.

Complete the picture

Can you find where these shapes fit in the main picture? Write the number of the space next to the piece.

a

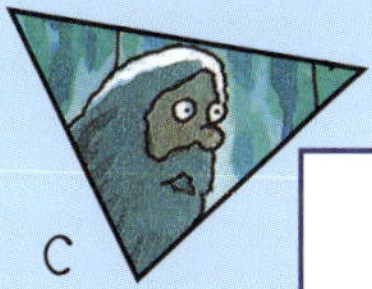
c

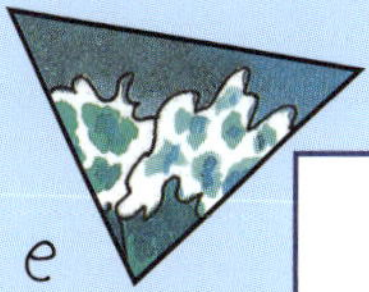
e

b

d

Joshua and the battle of Jericho

God chose Joshua to be the next leader of His people.

'Don't be afraid, Joshua,' said God. 'I will be with you wherever you go.'

On their way to the promised land, the Israelites had to pass through the city of

Jericho. The city had tall walls and strong city gates and lots of guards.

God told Joshua what to do: 'Tell seven priests to march around Jericho once every day for six days. On the seventh day they must march around the city seven times while the priests blow their special trumpets. And at the last trumpet blast, everyone must shout as loudly as they can.'

Everyone obeyed God – and the walls of the city fell down with a CRASH!

How many priests?

Write the number of priests on this page in the box.

How many have yellow belts?

How many have blue belts?

Maze

Help the priest find his way into Jericho.

Samuel's sleepless night

'Please, God, give me a baby,' Hannah prayed again and again. God heard her prayers and baby Samuel was born.

When Samuel was old enough, Hannah took him to stay with Eli the priest. Samuel would help the old man serve God.

One night, when Samuel was in bed, he heard a voice call, 'Samuel! Samuel!'

'Here I am,' said Samuel, running to Eli.

'I did not call you' said Eli. 'Go back to bed.'

So Samuel went back to bed.

It happened again. And Eli sent Samuel back to bed.

And again...

This time, Eli said, 'God is calling you, Samuel. Next time

say, "Speak, Lord, Your servant is listening!" '

So Samuel went back to bed.

'Samuel! Samuel!' came the voice.

'Speak, Lord, Your servant is listening!' said Samuel.

God told Samuel many things about the people of Israel.

Everything God said came true.

Spot the differences

Find eight differences between the two pictures and draw a circle around each of them.

Dot-to-dot

Join the dots from 1 to 27, to find something which helped Samuel see at night.

The shepherd boy

Farmer Jesse had eight sons. The youngest, David, was a shepherd. He took care of his father's sheep and kept them safe from wild animals.

One day the prophet Samuel visited Jesse. God had told him to choose one of Jesse's sons to be the next king.

Jesse brought seven of his sons to Samuel, but none of them was the one God had chosen.

'Have you any more sons?' asked Samuel.

'Yes,' said Jesse. 'Young David is looking after the sheep. I'll send for him.'

When Samuel saw David he heard God's voice saying, 'He is the one I want to be king.'

So Samuel poured oil on David's head to show that God had chosen him. From that day David knew God was always with him.

But there was a king already. His name was Saul. He didn't do as God wanted any more. He knew this was wrong and this made him sad.

Later David and King Saul became friends. David would play his harp to cheer up the king.

King Saul didn't know that David would be the next king of Israel.

Find the pair

Only two of these pictures of David are exactly the same.

Put a tick next to the two that match.

Complete the picture

Colour in the hats and head dresses in the picture below.

David and the giant

David's brothers had gone to fight the Philistines. They were soldiers in King Saul's army. One day, David went to visit them.

Suddenly he heard a man shouting loudly. It was Goliath the giant, the Philistine's biggest and strongest soldier. Everyone in King Saul's army was scared of Goliath.

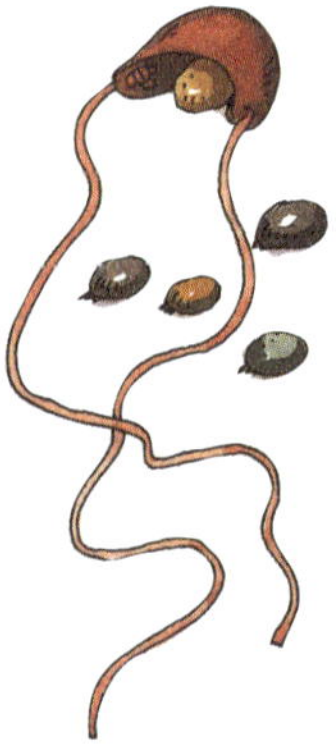

'I'm not afraid of this man!' said David. 'I will fight him!'

Carrying his sling, David picked up five stones from a stream. He walked towards Goliath.

The giant gave a nasty laugh when he saw little David. 'You have a sword and a spear,' said David, 'but God is on my side!'

David put a stone in his sling, whizzed it around his head and let go. The stone hit Goliath's forehead and he fell to the ground with a THUD!

The terrified Philistines ran away as fast as they could! God had given David the victory.

Find the words

Can you find these words hidden in the grid?

Draw a circle around each word.

Spear

Stone

David

a	s	t	o	n	e	m
p	w	c	p	d	t	n
g	o	l	i	a	t	h
x	r	a	b	v	a	b
w	d	s	l	i	n	g
m	a	v	x	d	p	t
s	p	e	a	r	o	x

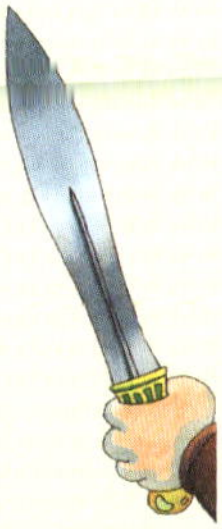

Sword

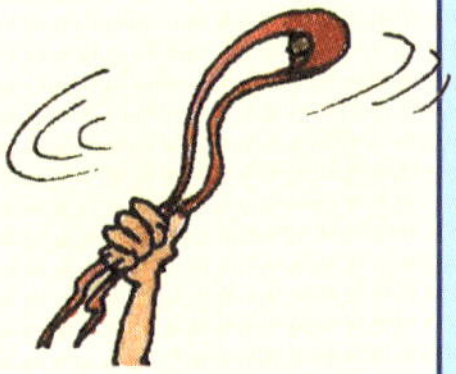

Sling

Goliath

Count the spears

How many of the soldiers in the picture are carrying spears?

How many of the soldiers have no spear?

How many soldiers are there in the picture?

God looks after Elijah

One day God sent the prophet Elijah to see King Ahab. He worshipped the false god of Baal.

'Change your ways. Be a good king,' Elijah warned the king or God won't let it rain.' said Elijah.

Ahab would not change. The country was dry. There was no water.

God sent ravens with bread and meat for Elijah to eat. God made sure he had water to drink.

Later God sent Elijah to a kind woman.

She had very little left to eat and there was still

no rain, but the woman shared her last loaf of bread with Elijah. Now she had no more flour and oil.

'Don't worry,' said Elijah. 'God says your flour and oil will never run out until the day it rains again!'

Sure enough, there was always enough to feed them! God looked after Elijah.

Big and small

Put a **B** next to the biggest raven and an **S** by the smallest.

Find the objects

Find these things in the big picture and draw a circle round them.

Trees

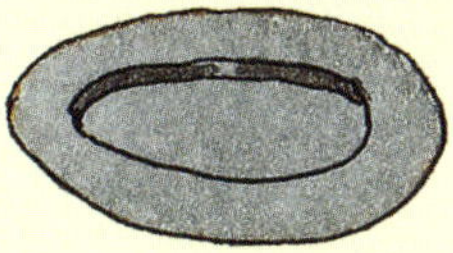

Plate

Bread

Elijah

Cup

Bowl

Fire from heaven

It had not rained for three years. God sent Elijah back to King Ahab.

'God is going to show you who is the true God,' Elijah said to the King.

'We will have a competition. Tell the prophets of Baal to come to Mount Carmel. They will put a bull on their altar. I will put another bull on the altar of the Lord. We will call on the one true God to send fire – and see who answers!'

The prophets of Baal shouted all day, but no fire came.

'Shout louder!' said Elijah. 'Baal isn't listening! Or maybe he's not there!'

Still Baal did not answer.

Then Elijah asked his servants to pour water on the altar. Soon it was soaking wet.

'Please God, show these people that You are the true God of Israel!' Elijah prayed loudly.

Whoosh! Fire flashed down heaven and burnt up everything on Elijah's altar!

Everyone was amazed and shouted, 'The Lord is God!'

Match the picture

Only one of these prophets is exactly like the one in the box.

Put a tick (✔) next to him.

Colours

Trace the word for each answer.

Elijah's robe is: red

Elijah's head dress is: green

The prophets' hats are: blue

The flames are: red and yellow

Naaman and the little servant girl

There was a little girl who was taken from Israel to be a servant in Syria. She worked for Naaman, a brave soldier in the Syrian army.

Naaman fell ill. His skin turned white and sore and no one could help.

The little girl said, 'Go and see God's prophet Elisha! He can make you better!'

So Naaman went to see Elisha.

Elisha said, 'Go and wash seven times in the River Jordan.'

Naaman was angry. 'The rivers in Syria are just as good.'

'Just try it and see,' said Naaman's servants.

So Naaman went down to the river. He dipped himself in it seven times – and his skin was soft and pink again!

Naaman went back to Elisha and said, 'Now I know that there is no god but the God of Israel.'

Find the ducks

How many ducks can you see in the picture? Draw a circle round each of them and write the number in the box.

Maze

Help Naaman find his way to the River Jordan.

Daniel in the lions' den

Daniel had been taken as a prisoner to a far-off country. But Daniel still trusted God and prayed to Him each day.

Daniel worked hard in the king's court. The king liked Daniel and this made people jealous.

'Make a law,' his enemies said to the King. 'People must pray to no one but you – or they will be thrown to the lions.'

And that's what the King did.

But Daniel still prayed to God. His enemies told the King, so Daniel had to be thrown to the hungry lions.

The King worried about Daniel all night.

In the morning the King ran to the lions' pit.

'Daniel!' he called.

'The lions didn't hurt me!' Daniel called. 'God sent an angel to shut their mouths.'

The King was very happy and he set Daniel free again, and he sent his enemies into the lions' pit instead!

Colour the dots

Colour in all the shapes marked with a dot to find out what is hiding in the cave.

Write down the answer in the box.

Count the lions

How many times can you find the word 'lion' in the grid below? ☐

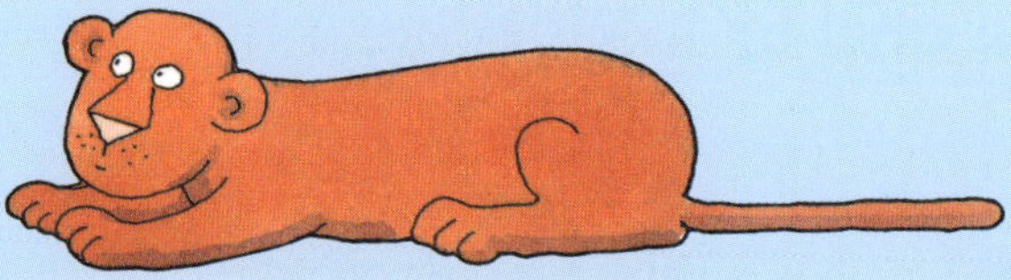

x	l	a	w	v	l
l	i	o	n	a	i
m	o	p	l	w	o
r	n	l	i	o	n
v	p	s	o	t	a
l	i	o	n	x	w

Jonah runs away

God spoke to Jonah: 'Go to Nineveh! Tell everyone there that I know all the bad things they are doing!'

But Jonah did not do as God asked. He was afraid. He ran away and got on a ship sailing far away.

Jonah settled down to sleep.

While he was sleeping God sent a big storm.

The wind blew. The waves splashed higher and higher.

All the sailors were very scared.

'Wake up!' they said to Jonah. 'We're going to sink!'

Jonah shouted, 'It's my fault! I ran from God. You must throw me overboard!'

So the sailors threw him into the sea. The storm stopped – the sailors were safe again.

Jonah was sinking deep into the sea when

God sent a huge fish to gobble him up!

Inside the fish Jonah prayed to God. 'I'm sorry that I didn't obey You.'

Three days later, the fish spat Jonah out onto the beach.

'Go to Nineveh,' God said again.

This time Jonah obeyed. The people of Nineveh listened to him and turned back to God.

Colour the picture

Colour in this picture of Jonah being thrown into the sea.

Find the fish

How many huge fish can you find in the sea?

Solutions to the puzzles from the Old Testament

God makes a world Pages 12 - 13

• The differences are circled on the picture.

Everything goes wrong Pages 16 - 17

• 1 frog; 2 rabbits; 3 blue flowers; 1 crocodile

• apple, cherries, banana

Noah's ark Pages 20 - 21

• The words are circled in the grid.

a	g	h	p	w	v
l	i	o	n	x	a
f	m	r	p	i	g
o	a	s	m	d	a
x	p	e	o	w	l
d	o	g	v	w	m

Rain, rain and more rain Pages 24 - 25

Abraham moves to Canaan pages 28 - 29

• There are 13 sheep.

Baby Isaac Pages 32 - 33

- There are 12 stars.
- The odd one out is circled on the picture.

Jacob plays a trick Pages 36 - 37

- The answers are circled on the picture.

Joseph's special coat Pages 40 - 41

- There are 8 sheep in the picture.

There are 10 brothers in the picture.

A slave in Egypt Pages 44 - 45

- The answers are circled on the picture.

- 3 red parcels., 4 blue parcels, 5 yellow parcels.

A baby in a basket Pages 48 - 49

Let My people go Pages 52 - 53

- 2 frogs, 4 frogs, 3 frogs, 5 frogs and 6 frogs.
- Picture 2 is the odd one out.

The great escape Pages 56 - 57

• The answers are circled on the pictures

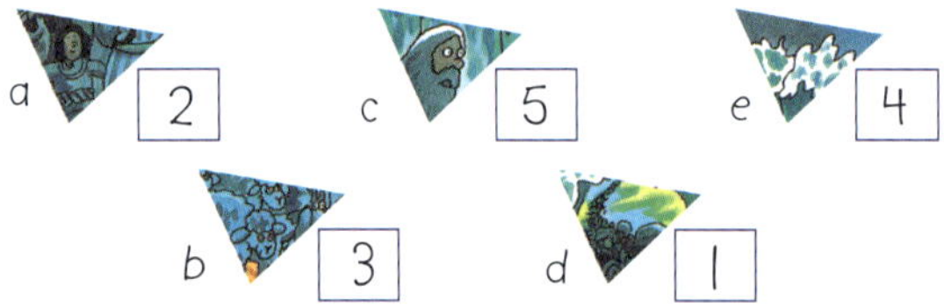

Joshua and the battle of Jericho Pages 60 - 61

• The are 7 priests.
3 are wearing yellow belts.
4 are wearing blue belts.

Samuel's sleepless night Pages 64 - 65

• The answers are circled on the picture.

The shepherd boy Pages 68 - 69

Drawings 1 and 2 are the same.

David and the giant Pages 72 - 73

• The answers are circled in the grid.

a	s	t	o	n	e	m
p	w	c	p	d	t	n
g	o	l	i	a	t	h
x	r	a	b	v	a	b
w	d	s	l	i	n	g
m	a	v	x	d	p	t
s	p	e	a	r	o	x

• 6 soldiers are carrying spears.
4 soldiers have no spears.
There are 10 soldiers in the picture.

God looks after Elijah Pages 76 - 77

• The answers are circled on the picture.

Fire from heaven Pages 80 - 81

Naaman and the little servant girl Pages 84 - 85

• There are 5 ducks in the picture.

Daniel in the lion's den Pages 88 - 89

• A lion is hiding in the cave.

• The word 'lion' appears 6 times in the grid; they are circled below.

x	l	a	w	v	l
l	i	o	n	a	i
m	o	p	l	w	o
r	n	l	i	o	n
v	p	s	o	t	a
l	i	o	n	x	w

Jonah runs away Pages 92 - 93

• There are 6 huge fish in the sea.

The New Testament

Mary's baby

Mary and Joseph lived in Nazareth. Soon they were going to be married.

One day Mary had a big surprise – the angel Gabriel visited her.

'Mary, don't be afraid,' said the angel. 'God has chosen you to have a baby boy. His name is Jesus. He is

God's Son and promised King.'

Mary was amazed. But she wanted to obey God.

'I will do what God wants,' she said.

One day Joseph had bad news.

'We must go to Bethlehem, where my family comes from. The Roman ruler wants to count everyone.'

Mary and Joseph arrived in Bethlehem after a long journey. But there was nowhere to stay in the busy little town. When Mary's baby was born she made a bed for Him in a manger.

Find and count

How many mice can you find in the picture? ☐

Complete the pictures

All these creatures have something missing.

Draw in the owl's beak.

Draw the ears on the donkey.

Draw the horns on the ox.

The angel and the shepherds

On the hills near Bethlehem, shepherds were looking after their sheep. Suddenly, the sky was filled with a blinding light and they saw an angel!

'Don't be afraid!' said the angel. 'I have good news for you! Tonight in Bethlehem God's promised King has been born! You will find the baby lying in a manger.'

Then the sky was filled with more angels, praising God. It was a wonderful sight!

At once, the shepherds left their sheep

and hurried off to Bethlehem.

'We must go to see this special baby!' they said.

They found Mary and Joseph, and the baby lying in the manger. 'It's all just as the angel said!' they exclaimed.

The shepherds went back to their sheep, singing songs of praise to God for the wonderful things they had seen.

Wordsearch

Draw a circle around the words the angel said to the shepherds.

afraid good news baby king manger

m	o	d	b	k	p
a	f	r	a	i	d
n	s	k	b	n	s
g	r	t	y	g	s
e	g	o	o	d	a
r	a	n	e	w	s

Join the dots

Join the dots to see what the shepherd is carrying.

How many sheep can you count on this page? ☐

The journey of the wise men

Far from Bethlehem some wise men were studying the stars.

They had spotted a new star, shining brightly in the sky.

'It means a new king has been born!' they said. 'We must travel to find Him. We will take gifts to honour Him!'

So the wise men packed their bags and set off, always following the star.

After a very long journey, the wise men reached Bethlehem.

'Look! The star is shining over that house!' they said excitedly.

They went quietly into the house and found Mary, Joseph and baby Jesus.

The wise men knelt down before the baby and worshipped Him.

'We have found the new King!' they said.

Then they gave Jesus precious gifts: gold, frankincense and myrrh.

Mary looked at the gifts in wonder and amazement.

Missing gifts

The wise men have their gifts hidden on their clothes. Draw a circle round them when you find them, and colour them in.

Maze

Show the wise man the correct way to reach the star over the house where he will find the baby Jesus.

The four fishermen

Jesus grew up and began to talk to people about God. Crowds of people came to listen.

One day, Jesus asked two fishermen for help. He wanted everyone to see Him and hear Him. So the fishermen – Simon and Andrew – let Jesus stand in their boat.

When Jesus had finished speaking, He told Simon to push the boat out and let down the fishing nets.

'We were fishing all night but caught nothing,' said Simon. But he did what Jesus said and suddenly the nets were

full of slippery, shiny fish!

The nets were very heavy, so James and John – Simon's friends – came in another boat to help pull up the nets.

Simon was amazed. It was a miracle!

'Don't be afraid,' said Jesus. 'Follow Me!'

The four fishermen were Jesus' first disciples, His special friends.

Complete the picture

Each of these details belongs in the big picture. Write the number of the space next to the shape which goes there.

a

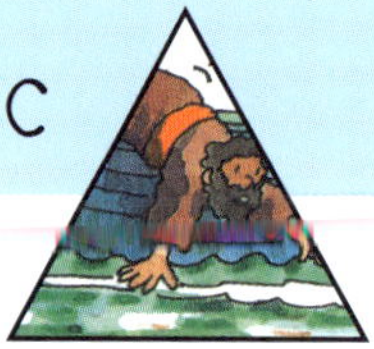
c

d

b

e

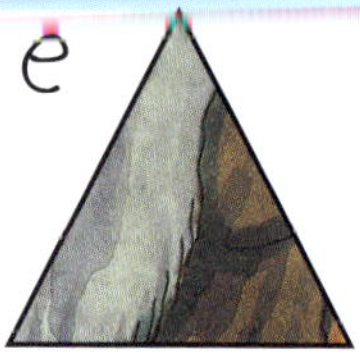
f

Which shapes are round?

Which shapes are square?

Which shapes are triangles?

Count the colours

Count the number of fish of each colour in the net.

How many red fish? ☐

How many *blue* fish? ☐

How many yellow fish? ☐

How many fish altogether? ☐

Jesus meets Matthew

One day, Matthew the tax collector had a visitor. It was Jesus.

Matthew was surprised. No one liked tax collectors. They often stole extra money for themselves. No one wanted to be Matthew's friend.

'Follow Me!' said Jesus.

At once, Matthew got up, left everything and became one of Jesus' special friends.

Matthew asked Jesus to a great feast in his house. There was wonderful food and wine.

It was a huge celebration.

'Why do you mix with *bad* people like tax collectors?' a man asked Jesus.

'I've come to help people who need Me,' he answered.

Matthew had spent his life counting money and taxes. Now he had left his money behind and was following Jesus.

Find the mistakes

Can you find six things which don't belong in this picture?
Mark them with a cross.

How much?

Tax collectors counted money.

Add up the coins in each of these sums.

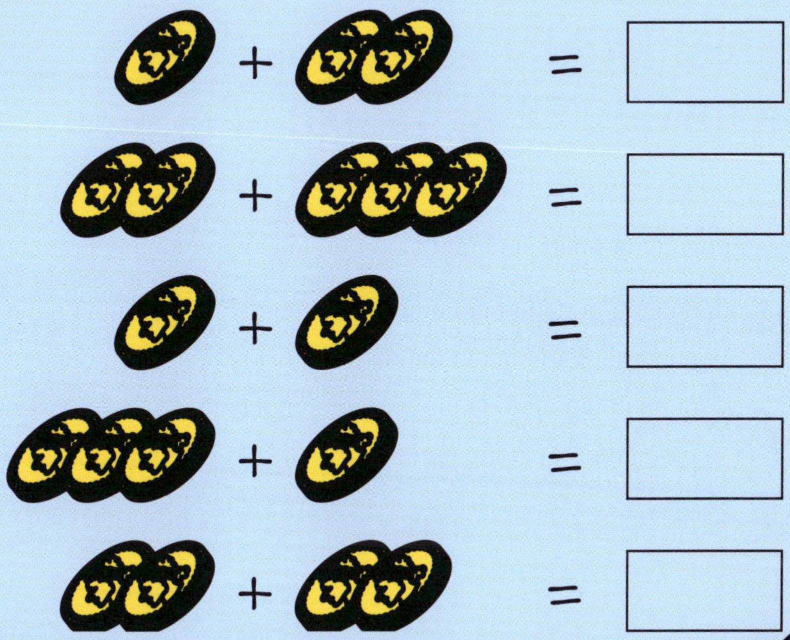

How many coins are there in the bag?

The four kind friends

There was a man who couldn't walk. His four friends carried him to see Jesus. He could make him well.

When they got to the house where Jesus was, they could not get in! There were too many people there. Then one friend had an idea.

'Let's go up to the roof,' he said.

The men carried their friend up the steps outside the house and pushed away the mud and branches on the roof until there was a big hole.

Then the men carefully lowered the man down in front of Jesus.

'Pick up your mat,' said Jesus. 'You can walk home by yourself now.'

The four friends smiled. Everyone was amazed. The man got up and went home. Jesus had made him well.

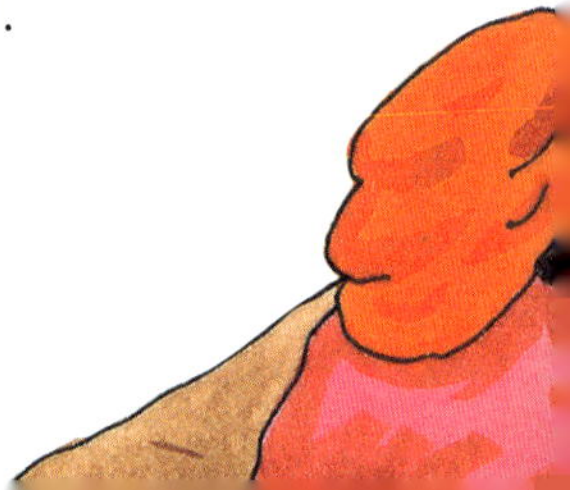

Which rope?

Only one of these ropes is still joined to the stretcher.

Which one is it? ☐

Spot the difference

Can you mark seven differences between these two pictures?

The story of the two houses

Jesus told many stories to the crowds who followed Him. One day He told this story:

'If you listen to My words and obey them, you will be like a wise man who built his house upon a rock.

'Two men were building houses. It took the first one a long time. He built a strong stone house on firm rock foundations. He was wise.

'The other man was lazy. He quickly built a house on sand. He was foolish.

'One day the weather turned bad! The rain poured down, strong winds blew and the rivers flooded.

'The house on the rock stood firm. The wise man was happy, glad that he'd worked so hard.

'The foolish man saw cracks in his walls. The cracks grew bigger and bigger ... then the house on the sand fell down with a CRASH!

'Be like the wise man,' said Jesus. 'Listen to My words and do what I say, and you will be safe.'

Maze

Help the wise man and the foolish man find the way to their own houses.

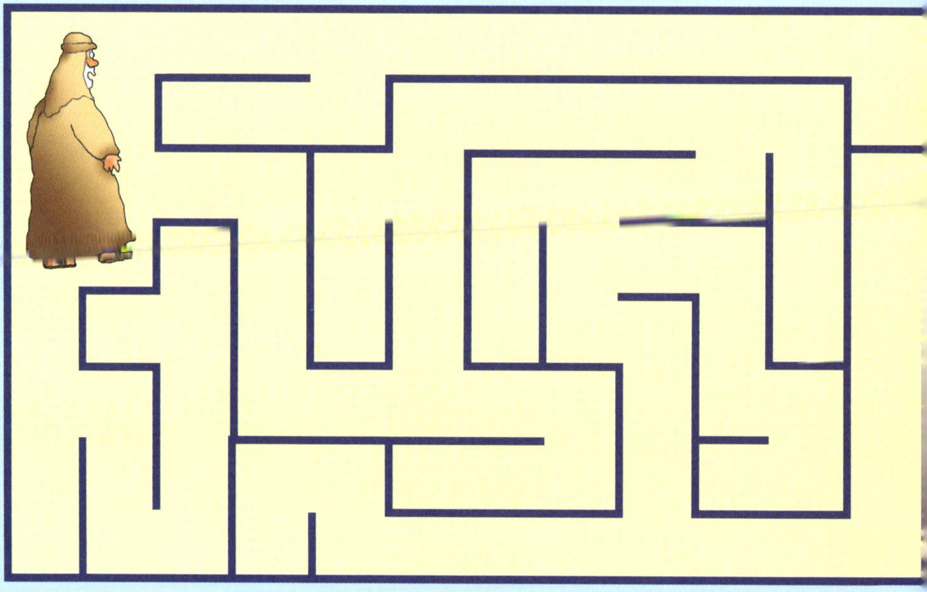

Opposites

Draw a line to link those words which have opposite meanings in the story.

rock	fell down
long time	foolish
wise	sand
stood firm	quickly

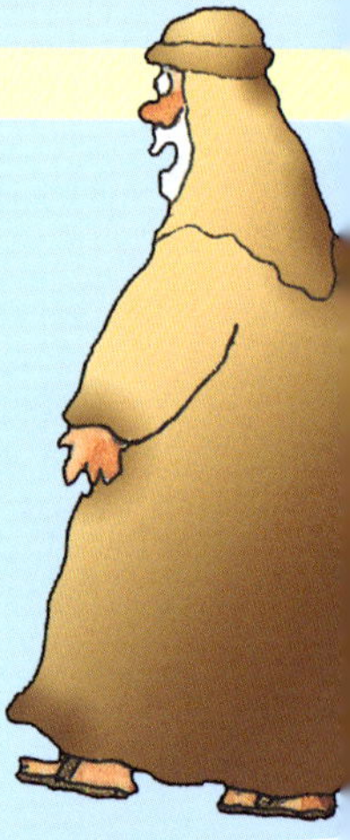

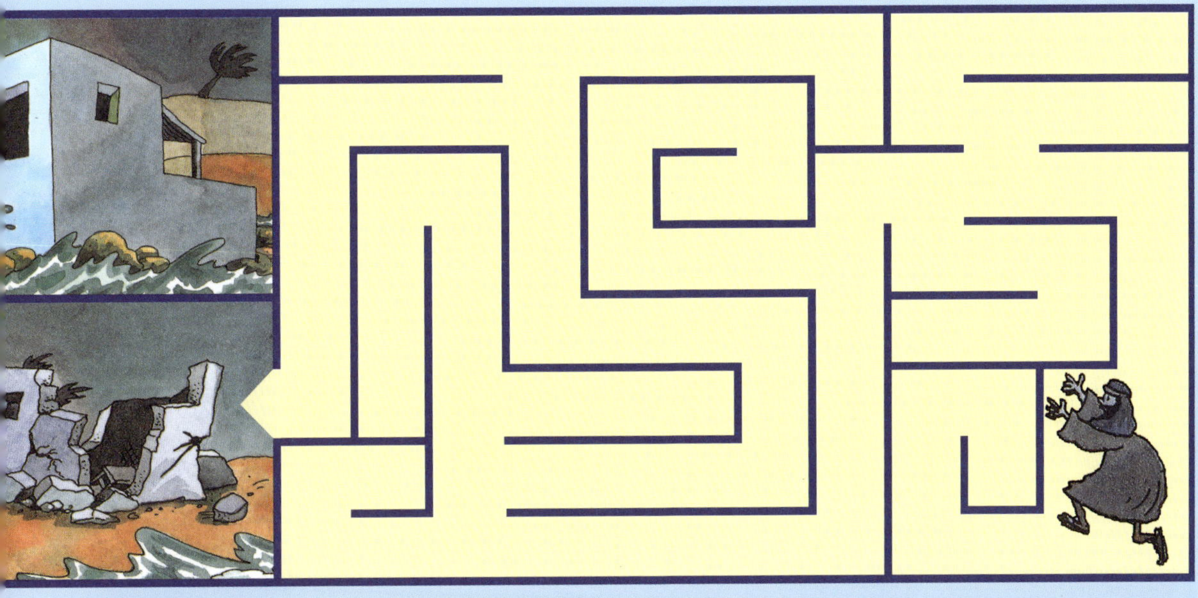

The big storm

'Let's sail to the other side of the lake,' said Jesus to His friends one day.

He was tired and soon fell asleep in the boat.

Suddenly a huge storm started. The little boat was rocked about and began to fill with water!

Jesus didn't notice the storm. He was still fast asleep.

'Wake up! Wake up!' the frightened disciples called to Jesus. 'We're going to sink!'

Jesus woke up. Then He stood up and said, 'Wind, be quiet. Waves, calm down.'

At once the storm vanished.

'Look, even the winds and waves obey Him!' said the disciples in amazement.

Who's there?

Which of these people sailed in the boat? Put a tick next to them.

a

b

c

d

e

f

Wordsearch

Find the words about storms in the grid. Which word means the opposite of a storm? Mark it on the grid in red.

storm wind calm rain wave water

s	t	o	r	m	v
m	o	c	a	l	m
r	s	w	i	n	d
a	w	a	v	e	s
i	w	a	t	e	r
n	c	k	a	m	s

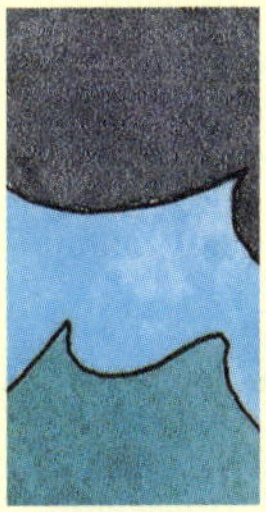

The girl who came back to life

One day, a man called Jairus called out from the crowd: 'Jesus! Please help me! My only daughter is dying!'

On the way to Jairus' house they met one of his servants.

'It's too late,' said the servant. 'The girl is dead.'

But Jesus said, 'Don't be afraid. Trust Me and she will be well.'

Everyone at Jairus' house was crying – they were very sad.

'Don't worry,' said Jesus kindly, 'she is not dead. She is just sleeping.'

He took the girl's hand and gently said, 'Get up, My child.'

She sat up at once! It was a miracle.

Her parents could hardly believe their eyes. They were very happy and they thanked Jesus with all their hearts.

Left or right?

Write '**r**' in the box next to the right hands and '**l**' in the box next to the left hands.

Top and bottom

Draw a line to match the heads to the bodies of the people from the big picture.

The big picnic

A huge crowd of people had been listening to Jesus all day. The sun was beginning to go down and everyone was hungry.

'Give them something to eat,' Jesus said to His disciples.

'There's a young boy here with five loaves and two fish,' said Andrew. 'That will never be enough.'

Jesus took the loaves and fish, gave thanks to God, and broke them into pieces.

His friends shared out the food among the

crowd. It was like a big picnic.

To everyone's amazement there was plenty for everyone. No one went hungry!

Later the disciples gathered up enough leftovers to fill twelve baskets.

Everyone was amazed at what Jesus had done.

Large, small and odd one out

Put a tick next to the biggest loaf and the biggest fish.

Put a cross next to the smallest loaf and the smallest fish.

How many loaves are there in this puzzle?

How many fish can you see here?

Which is the odd fish out?

Colour in the picture

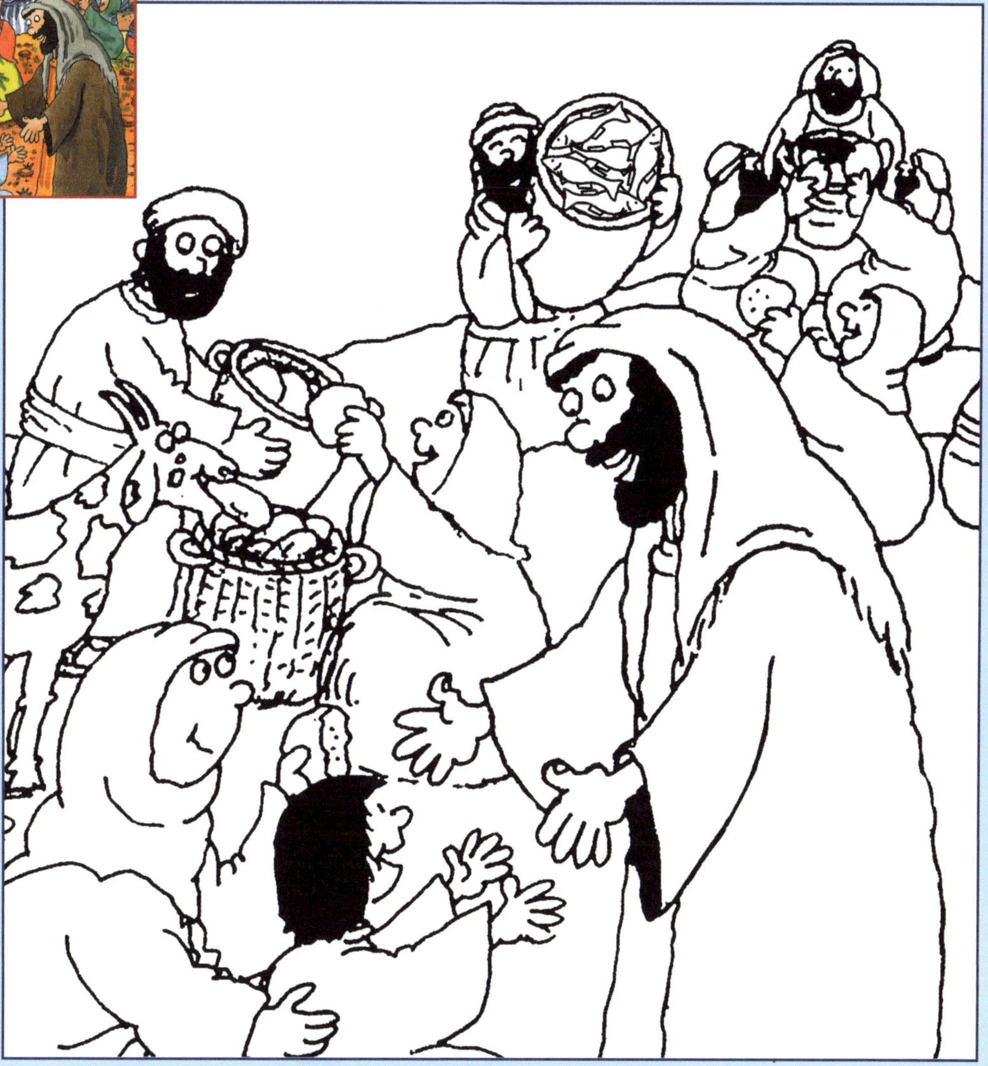

The good neighbour

Jesus told this story about how to be kind to other people

'A man was going down the lonely road from Jerusalem to Jericho. Suddenly robbers jumped out from behind a rock. They took his money and his clothes and hurt him very badly. The poor man couldn't move.

'Then he heard footsteps.

'"Help, at last," thought the injured man. But the man walked on by.

'Later he heard more footsteps. "He will help me!" thought the man.

'But the second man walked past him too.

'Then a Samaritan came along the road. He rushed over to help.

'He bandaged the man's cuts and gave him a

drink of water. Then
he put the man on his donkey and
took him to an inn. He paid the innkeeper to take
care of the man.'

Then Jesus said, 'Go and be like that kind man.'

Spot the difference

These four donkeys all have one detail which is different from the other three. Put a circle around each difference.

Copy the word

Donkey

Join the dots

Who was watching the good neighbour help the injured man?

The story of the lost sheep

Jesus once told this story about a shepherd:

'A shepherd once had a hundred sheep. He knew them all, looked after them well and kept them safe from wild animals.

'One day, the shepherd found that one was missing! Where could it be?

'He left the other ninety-nine safely penned in the fold and set out to look for the lost sheep.

'He looked everywhere: beneath bushes, beside the stream and behind rocks. Suddenly he heard a faint "baa-aa".

'He rushed towards the sound. Yes, he had found his lost sheep!

'The shepherd put the lost sheep

on his shoulders and carried it carefully home.

'He was so pleased to find his sheep that he held a special party.

'God is a bit like that shepherd,' said Jesus. 'He cares if any one of His sheep is lost.'

Count the sheep

How many sheep can you count in this picture?

How many sheeps' ears can you see?

How many sheeps' legs can you see?

Maze

Help the shepherd return to the rest of the flock.

The man who could not see

A poor blind man sat begging at the roadside every day.

One day, he heard excited people saying: 'Jesus!' 'Let's see Jesus!' 'Jesus can heal people!'

'That's what I want,' thought the man.

He stood up and shouted out: 'Jesus! Take pity on me!'

'Be quiet!' people grumbled.

But Jesus stopped and asked kindly, 'What do you want Me to do for you?'

'I want to be able to see!' the man said.

'Then see!' said Jesus. 'You believe in Me and your faith has made you well!'

At once, the man's eyes became clear and he could see.

'Thanks be to God!' shouted the man. 'I can see! I can see!'

It was another of Jesus' miracles.

Find and count

One of the people below isn't in the crowd who saw the blind man made well.

Write their letter in the box. ☐

How many children can you see in the crowd? ☐

How many grown ups can you see in the crowd? ☐

a

b

c

d

Find the differences

Can you spot eight differences between these two pictures? Draw a circle around them when you find them.

The little tax collector

Zacchaeus was a tax collector in Jericho. No one liked him. He was a cheat and a thief.

One day, Zacchaeus heard that Jesus was coming to Jericho. He wanted to see Jesus.

Zacchaeus was very short. He couldn't see over the crowds of people waiting for Jesus.

'I'll climb a tree!' thought Zacchaeus. He clambered into the branches and watched.

Jesus came closer. Suddenly He stopped – right beneath the tree!

'Zacchaeus, hurry down!' said Jesus, 'I must come to your house today.'

Zacchaeus could hardly believe it. Why would Jesus want to speak to him?

He climbed down and they went to his house.

Jesus and Zacchaeus talked for a long time.

Afterwards he told Jesus, 'I will give away half of all I own and repay everyone I have cheated.'

Meeting Jesus had changed Zacchaeus for ever.

Where is he?

Zacchaeus is hidden in the trees. Draw a circle to show where he is.

Odd one out

Which of these people is different from all the others? Draw a circle around him.

Colours

The people are wearing colourful clothes. Draw a line to show;

a lady with a yellow robe	a man with a green head dress	a man in a brown coat	a man with a blue belt

The King on a donkey

It was time for a special festival called Passover. Jesus and lots of other people were going to Jerusalem to celebrate.

Jesus said to two friends, 'You will find a young donkey in the village. Untie it and bring it to me. You can tell the owner that you master needs it.'

The disciples did what Jesus said.

Then Jesus got on the donkey and rode into Jerusalem. Great crowds of people cheered for Jesus. They waved palm branches and spread their cloaks on the road.

'Hosanna!' they shouted. 'God bless the promised King! Glory to God!'

Jesus was welcomed into the city.

Path to Jerusalem

Draw a line to show Jesus a way to Jerusalem treading on red cloaks only.

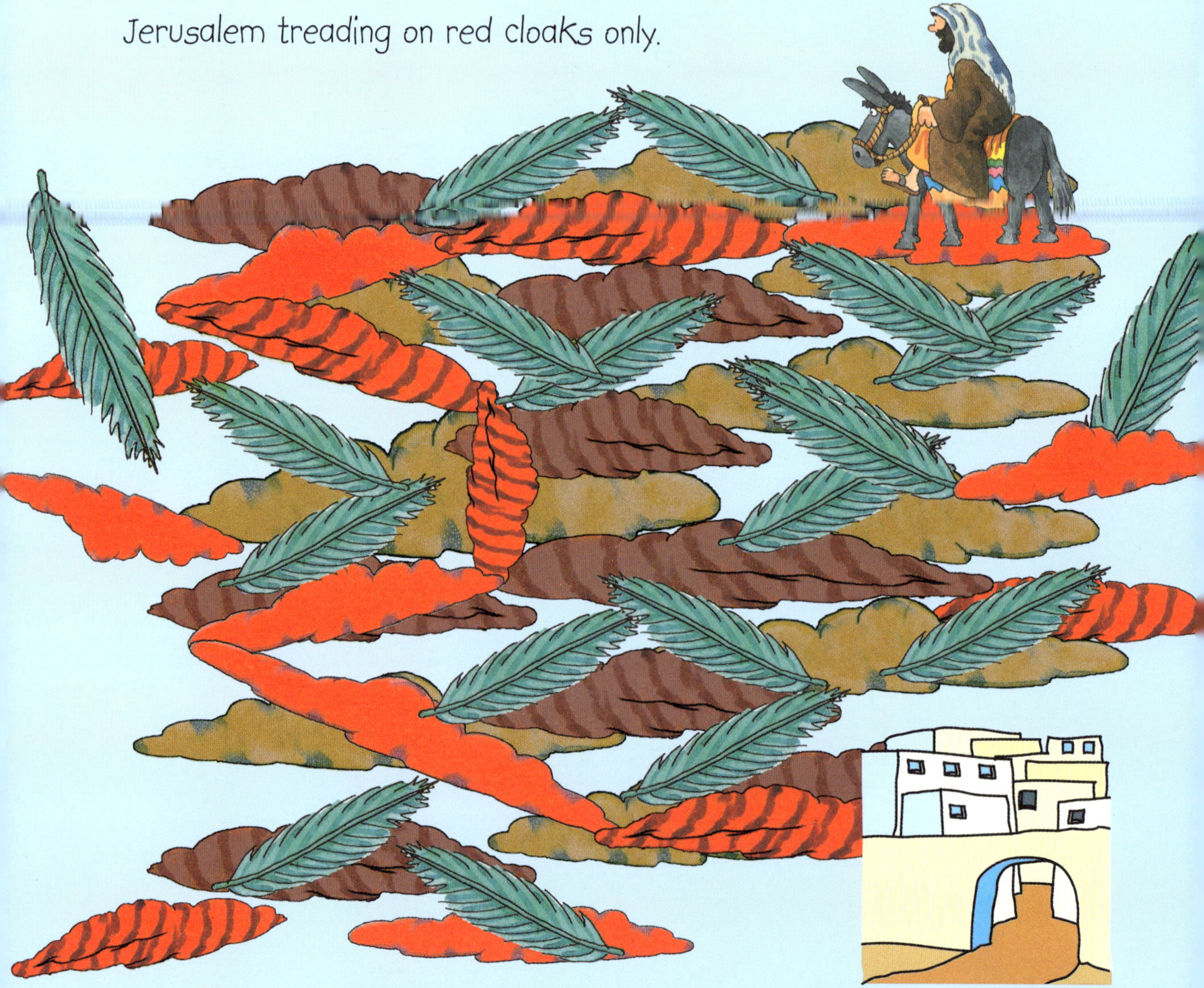

A blanket for the donkey

Colour in this blanket, following the guide to colours in the key below.

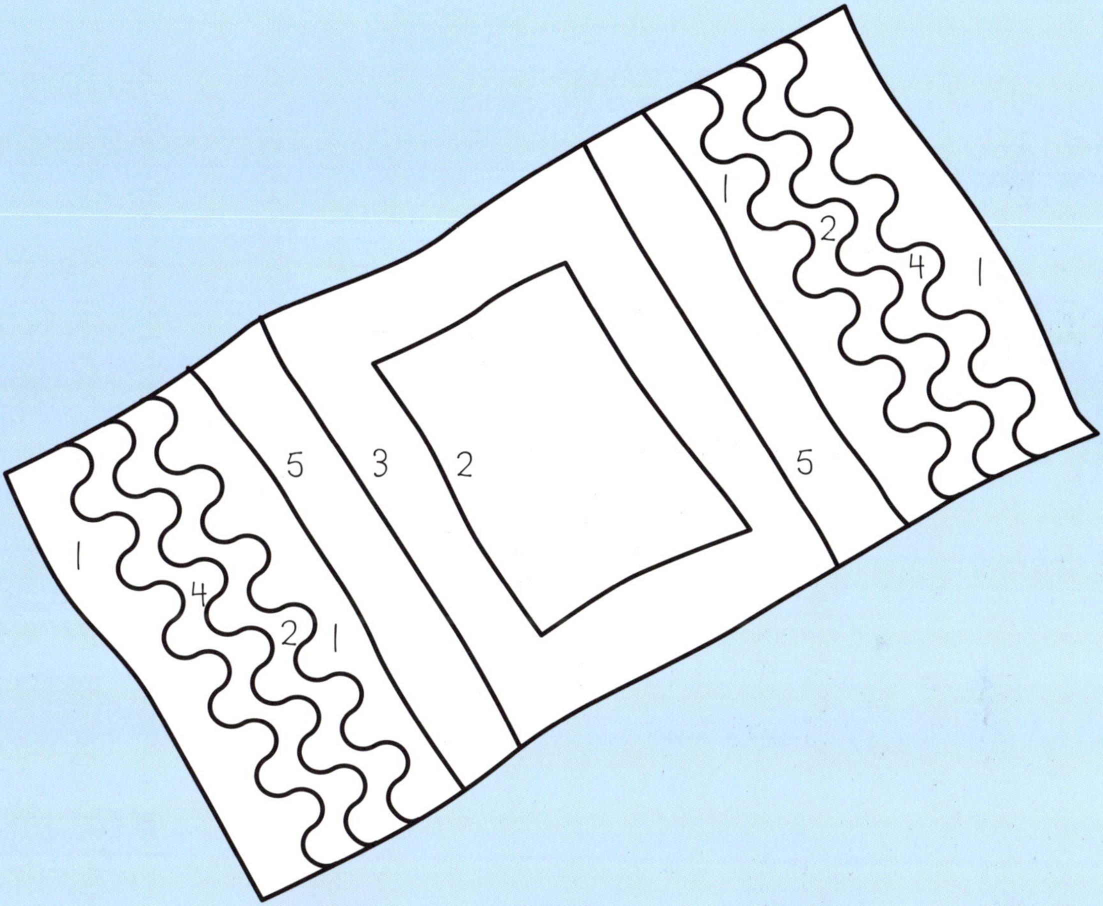

1 Yellow

2 Red

3 Green

4 Purple

5 Blue

Jesus dies on the cross

Jesus had many friends but He also had enemies. They wanted to get rid of Him. Jesus knew that He was going to die.

So Jesus shared one last special meal with His friends.

That night, He said things to help them remember Him. He wanted the disciples to understand why He had to die. When Jesus died He would put people right with God.

Later that night, Jesus was arrested. But He had done nothing wrong!

Cruel soldiers put a crown of thorns on Jesus' head. His enemies told lies about Him.

Jesus had to carry a heavy cross up a hill. Then He was put on the cross and left to die.

His mother Mary and His friends were very sad.

When Jesus' body was taken down from the cross it was put in a garden tomb. A big stone was rolled across the doorway.

It had been a terrible day.

Match the pairs

Draw a line to join each of the helmets that are exactly the same.

Find the crosses

Colour in the shapes with a dot. How many crosses can you find?

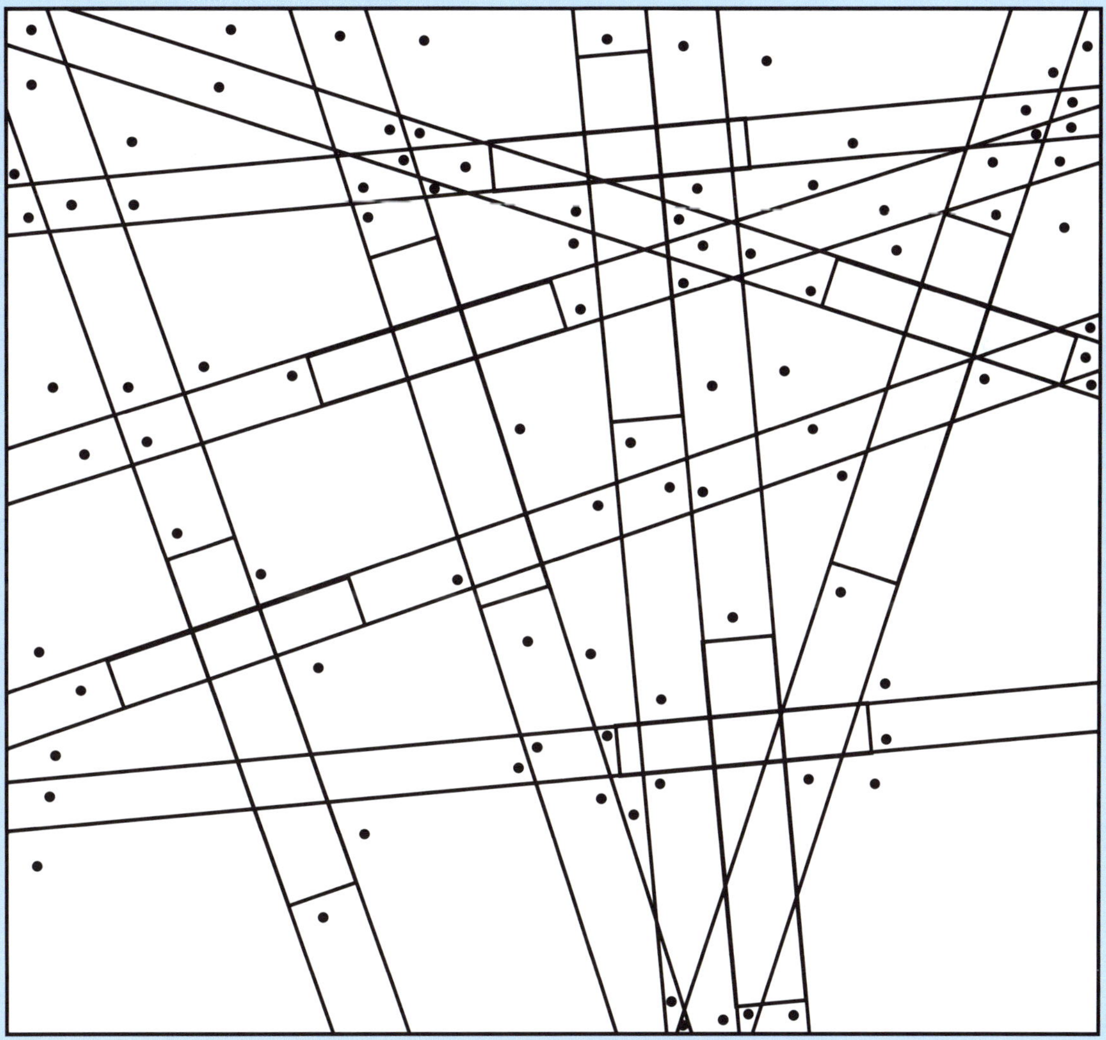

Jesus is alive

One morning, three days after Jesus had died, three of His friends went to the tomb. The women wanted to put sweet-smelling spices on Jesus' body.

When they reached the tomb, they had a big shock! The heavy stone had been rolled away.

The women were afraid. They looked into the tomb. The body was gone! Where was Jesus? Who had taken Him?

Suddenly they saw two men in bright shining clothes standing there.

'Why are you looking for Jesus here?' one man said. 'He is not dead, He is alive!

Full of excitement, the women ran to tell the disciples.

'Jesus is alive!' they said. 'The tomb is empty!'

The disciples couldn't believe the news. Peter and John ran to the tomb and, sure enough, Jesus was not there!

Mary Magdalene stayed in the garden. It was there that she met and talked with Jesus. He really was alive!

Missing letters

Fill in the missing letters to see what the women told the disciples.

J ___ ___ ___ s ___ s ___ l ___ ___ e!

Big and small

Put a **B** next to the biggest jar and an **S** next to the smallest one.

Find and count

Look at the picture below and find and count how many of these creatures you can find?

Thomas believes

Mary Magdalene was so excited! She told her friends about seeing Jesus, and later they saw Him for themselves. He suddenly appeared when they were in a locked room.

The disciples were filled with joy and amazement.

But one disciple, Thomas, was missing. His friends told him the good news, but Thomas did not believe it.

'But we have seen Him!' said his friends.

'Well, unless I can see the marks where He was nailed to the cross, I won't believe it,' answered Thomas.

A week later, all the disciples were gathered together again.

Suddenly Jesus was there in the room with them!

'Look at My hands and feet,' He said. 'Stop doubting, Thomas!' At last, Thomas believed that Jesus was alive.

Spot the difference

The pictures outside the box all have one detail that is different from the one inside. Mark each difference with a circle.

Complete the picture

Write the number that appears in the blank space next to the correct detail to complete the picture.

a

b

c

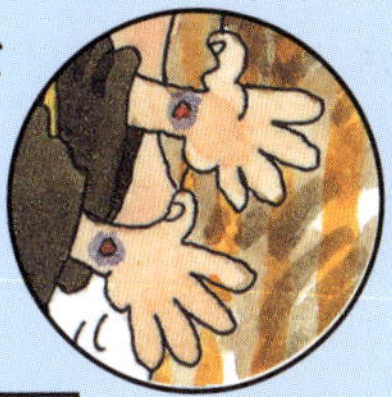

d

e

Breakfast on the beach

'Let's go fishing,' said Simon Peter early one morning. Six friends joined him and they pushed the boat out onto Lake Galilee.

They let down their nets into the water and waited... But they did not catch a single fish.

'Throw your net on the other side of the boat,' called a man on the beach. 'Then you will catch plenty of fish.'

So the fishermen threw their net on the other side. At once it was full of fish!

'That's Jesus!' said one of the fishermen.

Jesus was sitting by a charcoal fire on the beach.

'Come and eat!' He said.

The disciples were so pleased to see Jesus again.

Count and colour

Colour in the fish in the net, using a different colour for each type.

Count how many different types of fish have been caught. ☐

How many fish altogether are there in the net? ☐

Wordsearch

Can you mark all these words from the story in the grid?

fish

bird

sea

fire

beach

boat

b	o	a	t	w	b
i	s	s	m	r	e
r	t	w	s	e	a
d	p	d	q	c	c
m	n	f	i	s	h
f	i	r	e	t	x

Counting puzzle

How many seagulls can you count in the picture?

Jesus goes to heaven

One day Jesus told His friends something very important.

'Stay in Jerusalem,' He said, 'I will send you a special helper, God's Holy Spirit. Then you will be filled with power and will tell everyone about Me.

'You will want people all over the world to know about Me. You will tell them what I have taught you, and about My death and resurrection.'

Then Jesus was taken up to heaven, hidden in a cloud. Suddenly two men dressed in white stood beside the disciples.

'Why are you looking up at the sky?' they asked. 'Jesus will come back again in the same way as you saw Him go,' they promised.

Jesus' friends went back to Jerusalem. There was Peter, John, James and Andrew, Philip and

Thomas, Bartholomew and Matthew, James, Simon and Judas. Later, they chose Matthias, another follower of Jesus, to be in their group.

Mary, Jesus' mother, and other women who loved Jesus joined them. They all prayed to God and waited.

Spot the difference

Eight extra details appear in the bottom picture. Can you find them and mark them with a circle?

Picture maze

Can you help the two groups of people find their way to Jerusalem?

The good news of Jesus

One day, Jesus' special friends were praying together.

Whoosh! Suddenly a sound like blowing wind filled the room. Flickering flames touched everyone there and the friends found

they could speak in many languages.

This was what Jesus had promised – He had sent them His special helper, God's Holy Spirit. They were so happy!

They went out and told the crowds all about Jesus. And about how He had been put to death but come alive again!

People from other countries came to listen. And they wanted to become friends of Jesus too.

Jesus' friends and the new believers were so excited. They wanted to share the good news of Jesus with everyone.

Colours

Draw a line from each block of colour to something the same colour in the picture below.

yellow red blue green orange

How many people are wearing something yellow?

How many people are wearing something blue?

How many people are wearing something red?

Missing letters

Fill in the missing letters to complete the message the disciples gave to the crowds.

'I b _ _ _ _ g y _ _ _ _ _ _ d n _ _ _ _!'

What's wrong?

Can you find eight mistakes in the picture below?

Mark them with a circle.

Solutions to the puzzles from the New Testament

Mary's baby Pages 102-103

- There are 8 mice in the picture.

The angel and the shepherds Pages 106-107

- The words are circled on the grid.
- There are 6 sheep.

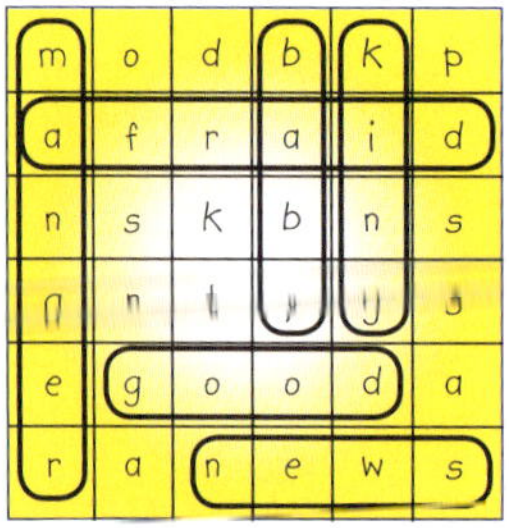

The journey of the wise men Pages 110-111

- The gifts are circled on the picture.

- The correct route is shown on the maze.

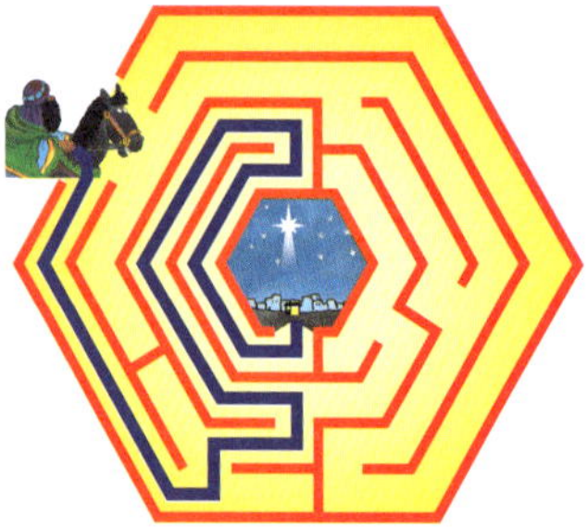

The four fishermen Pages 114-115

- a - 2; b - 4; c - 5; d - 3; e - 1; f - 6
- b and f are round, a and d are square, c and e are triangles.
- The are 3 red fish, 2 yellow fish, 4 blue fish and 9 fish altogether.

Jesus meets Matthew Pages 118-119

- The wrong things are circled on the picture.

- 1+2 = 3, 2+3 = 5, 1+1 = 2, 3+1 = 4, 2+2 = 4
- There are 8 coins in the bag.

The four kind friends Pages 122-123

- Rope 7 is still attached to the stretcher.
- The differences are circled on the picture.

The story of the two houses Pages 126-127

- The correct routes are shown on the maze.

- The word pairs are: rock - sand; wise - foolish; long time - quickly; stood firm - fell down

The big storm Pages 130-131

- Only characters a, c, d and e sailed in the boat.
- The opposite of 'storm' is 'calm'.

s	t	o	r	m	v
m	o	c	a	l	m
r	s	w	i	n	d
a	w	a	v	e	s
i	w	a	t	e	r
n	c	k	a	m	s

The girl who came back to life Pages 134-135

- There are 6 left hands and 6 right hands.
- The correct heads and bodies are shown below.

The big picnic Pages 138-139

- There are 7 loaves and 7 fishes.
- The odd fish is circled in red.

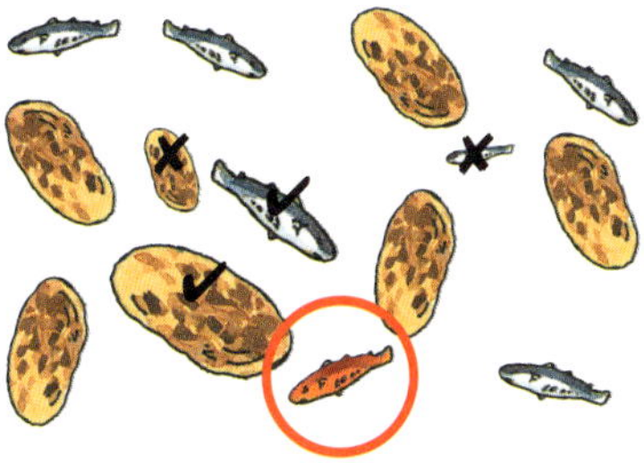

The good neighbour Pages 142-143

- The differences are circled on the pictures.

- A snake and a bird are watching the good neighbour.

The story of the lost sheep Pages 146-147

- There are 6 sheep in the picture. You can see 12 ears and 7 legs.
- The correct path is shown on the maze.

The man who could not see Pages 150-151

- Character c is not in the picture.
- There are 2 children and 17 grown-ups in the picture.
- The differences are ringed on the picture below.

The little tax collector Pages 154-155

- The character is circled on the picture.

- The odd one out is circled on the picture below.

The King on a donkey Pages 158-159

- The path is shown on the picture.

Jesus dies on the cross Pages 162-163

- The pairs of helmets are connected below.

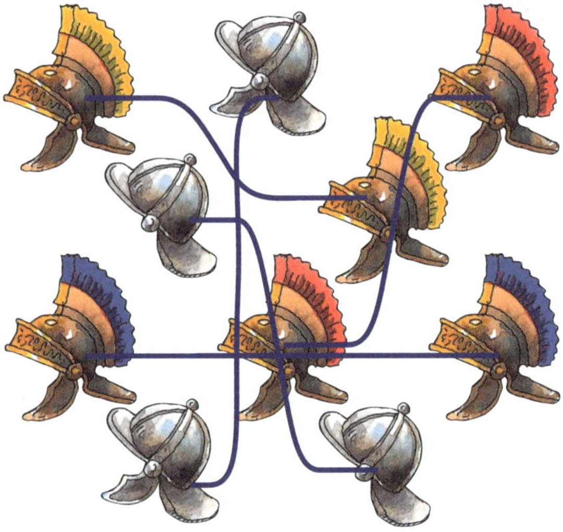

- There are 5 crosses in the drawing.

Jesus is alive Pages 166-167

• The women said **'Jesus is alive'**.

• The smallest and biggest jars are shown in the picture.

• There are 5 birds, 3 flies and 4 butterflies.

Thomas believes Pages 170-171

• The answers are circled on the pictures.

• The correct details are shown here.

Breakfast on the beach Pages 174-175

• 3 different types of fish are in the net. 9 fish have been caught all together.

• The words are circled on the grid below.

b	o	a	t	w	b
i	s	s	m	r	e
r	t	w	s	e	a
d	p	d	q	c	c
m	n	f	i	s	h
f	i	r	e	t	x

• There are 12 seagulls in the picture.

Jesus goes to heaven Pages 178-179

• The details are circled on the picture.

• The correct routes are shown on the maze.

The good news of Jesus Pages 182-183

• Three people are wearing yellow, seven people are wearing blue, six people are wearing red.

• The message reads **'I bring you good news'**

• The mistakes are circled on the picture.

Bible stories can be found as follows:

Old Testament

God makes a world Genesis 1:1-31

Everything goes wrong Genesis 2:8 – 3:24

Noah's ark Genesis 6:9 – 7:24

Rain, rain and more rain Genesis 8:1 – 9:17

Abraham's moves to Canaan Genesis 12:1-8; 13;1-2

Baby Isaac Genesis 15:4-5; 18:1-15; 21:1-3

Jacob plays a trick Genesis 25:21-34; 27:1-27

Joseph's special coat Genesis 37:1-11

A slave in Egypt Genesis 37:12-36; 45:1-7

The baby in the basket Exodus 2:1-10

Let My people go Exodus 5:1 – 12:31

The great escape Exodus 13:21 – 14:30

Joshua and the battle of Jericho Joshua 1:1-6; 6:1-20

Samuel's sleepless night 1 Samuel 3:1-21

The shepherd boy 1 Samuel 16:1-23

David and the giant 1 Samuel 17:1-50

God looks after Elijah 1 Kings 17:1-16

Fire from heaven 1 Kings 18:16-39

Naaman and the little servant girl 2 Kings 5:1-15

Daniel in the lions' den Daniel 6:1-24

Jonah runs away Jonah 1:1 – 3:10

New Testament

Mary's baby Luke 1:26-38; 2:1-7

The angels and the shepherds Luke 2:8-20

The journey of the wise men Matthew 2:1, 9-11

The four fishermen Luke 5:1-11

Jesus meets Matthew Matthew 9:9-13

The four kind friends Luke 5:17-26

The story of the two houses Luke 6:46-49

The big storm Mark 4:35-41

The girl who came back to life Luke 8:40-42, 49-56

The big picnic Matthew 14:13-21

The good neighbour Luke 10:25-37

The story of the lost sheep Luke 15:3-7

The man who could not see Luke 18:35-43

The little tax collector Luke 19:1-10

The king on a donkey Matthew 21:1-9

Jesus dies on a cross Luke 22:14-22; John 19:1-42

Jesus is alive John 20:1-9

Thomas believes John 20:19-29

Breakfast on the beach John 21:1-14

Jesus goes to heaven Acts 1:1-14

The good news of Jesus Acts 2:1-47

Bible Quiz

Can you answer these quiz questions? There is one question for each story. Look back at the stories if you need help.

1 Name the first people God created.

2 Who told Eve to eat the fruit?

3 What did Noah build?

4 What was the sign of God's promise?

5 Who left his home because God told him to?

6 What was the name of Abraham and Sarah's baby?

7 How many babies did Rebecca have?

8 Who tricked his father?

9 Who was Jacob's favourite son?

10 What did Joseph's brothers do to him?

11 Who pulled baby Moses from the river?

12 What was the first plague?

13 Which sea did the Israelites cross?

14 Where did the city walls fall down?

15 Who heard God speak in the night?

16 Who was Jesse's youngest son?

17 Who did David fight?

18 What brought food to Elijah?

19 What did God send from heaven?

20 Who washed seven times in the River Jordan?

21 Who was thrown to the lions?

22 What swallowed Jonah?

23 Who gave birth to the baby Jesus?

24 Where was Jesus born?

25 Who followed a star?

26 Which fishermen followed Jesus?

27 What job did Matthew do?

28 Who made a hole in the roof?

29 How many houses were there in Jesus' story?

30 Who calmed a storm?

31 Whose little girl was brought back to life?

32 What did Jesus use to feed thousands of people?

33 Who was a good neighbour?

34 What did the shepherd lose?

35 Why did Bartimaeus need help?

36 What did Zacchaeus do to see Jesus?

37 What did Jesus ride into Jerusalem?

38 Why was the tomb empty?

39 Which disciple doubted that Jesus was alive?

40 Who shouted to the fishermen from the shore?

41 Where did Jesus go after his resurrection?

42 Who came on the Day of Pentecost?

The answers are on page 192.

Bible Quiz Answers

1 Adam and Eve.
2 A snake.
3 An ark.
4 A rainbow.
5 Abraham.
6 Isaac.
7 Two, twin boys.
8 Jacob.
9 Joseph.
10 Sold him as a slave
11 An Egyptian princess.
12 River Nile turns to blood.
13 The Red Sea.
14 Jericho.
15 Samuel.
16 David.
17 Goliath.
18 Ravens.
19 Fire.
20 Naaman.
21 Daniel.
22 A big fish.
23 Mary.
24 Bethlehem.
25 The wise men.
26 Simon, Andrew, James and John.
27 He was a tax collector.
28 Four friends.
29 Two houses.
30 Jesus.
31 Jairus.
32 Five loaves and two fish.
33 The good Samaritan.
34 A sheep.
35 He was blind and couldn't see.
36 He climbed a tree.
37 A donkey.
38 Jesus had been raised from the dead.
39 Thomas.
40 Jesus.
41 Heaven.
42 The Holy Spirit.